QUIRKY
COMIC VERSE &
mondegreen
MISCHIEF

QUIRKY
COMIC VERSE &
mondegreen
MISCHIEF

Keith Kemp

First published 2025

Copyright © Keith Kemp 2025

The right of Keith Kemp to be identified as the author of this work has been asserted in accordance with the Copyright, Designs & Patents Act 1988.

All rights reserved. No part of this book may be reproduced, stored in a retrieval system, or transmitted in any form or by any means, digital, electronic, electrostatic, magnetic tape, mechanical, photocopying, recording or otherwise, without the written permission of the copyright holder.

Published under licence by Brown Dog Books and
The Self-Publishing Partnership Ltd, 10b Greenway Farm, Bath Rd, Wick,
nr. Bath BS30 5RL, UK

www.selfpublishingpartnership.co.uk

ISBN printed book: 978-1-83952-974-0

Cover design by Andrew Prescott
Internal design by Andrew Easton

Printed and bound in the UK

This book is printed on FSC® certified paper

To Anthea, my best friend and wife of nearly 60 years without whom this little book would not have been possible.

Contents

Turn to the Right	8
Goblins	10
Asparagus Tongs	12
Goldfish Perspective	14
Macho Male	19
Customer Service	22
Picture Hanging	24
Senior Citizen	28
Bantams	31
Sunbathing	33
If I had wings	34
Not Oven Ready	36
An Evolutionary Tale	37
Jack Spratt	38
Spring	39

Mondegreens

Introduction to Mondegreens	40
The Countess of Ayr	41
Doing Bird	41
Canny Scots	41
Ecclesiastical Archery	42
Dressing Down	42
Devotional	42

First Aid	43
Less and Less	43
Best avoided if	43
Snug Solution	44
Camping	44
Ha Ha Grandpa	44
A Door	45
The Fromes	45
The Allium Clan	45
Mondegreen Key	46
Taxing	48

Turn to the Right

I just wanted to travel from 'A' to 'B'
But my satnav app would not speak to me.
It displayed a map showing where I should go
But it was too small. The names didn't show.

I did what I could with tweak after tweak
But in vain, I fear, as it just would not speak.
It progressively seemed I'd been sold a pup
As try as I might it would not speak up.

I don't like to admit to being defeated
But hard as I tried I just couldn't beat it.
So, tail between legs, I gave up in disgust
Keeping old map skills is really a 'must'.

The route was a little bit tricky to see
But in due course I got to my 'B'.
Then, in the wee small hours of the night
A firm voice instructed me: 'Turn to the right.'

I woke with a start wondering what had occurred.
It took me a moment to see how absurd
The app had become. How badly behaved
Its conduct was gross, little short of depraved.

But perhaps I'd messed up with some mapping trap
Or had I bought into a misaligned app?
To settings I went – looked up Siri and Search
To determine why I'd been left in the lurch.

WiFi and Bluetooth, Aeroplane Mode
Everything normal. No problems showed.
Unmute was on but still not a peep
I considered my options and went back to sleep.

Goblins

I've lost my diary. Where's my pen?

The goblins have got out again.

It is the goblins' great delight

To spirit away out of sight

The very moment that they're able

Things I put down on the table.

They really are a wretched curse.

I'm glad I do not have a purse

They'd have it off me just like that.

They even 'lost' a favourite hat.

The trouble is they've never been

Caught in the act. I've never seen

A sneaky goblin's hand reach out

In time for me to give a shout

To frighten him or her away

With a 'Desist. You must not stay.'

I must be fair. They never steal

Just rearrange and don't reveal

That well-placed paper sure obscures

Most of the things that one procures.

Clearly a behavioural lapse.

And I've considered that perhaps

It's absolutely not absurd

That by them I am being observed.

And that there are goblin debates

To exploit my weaker traits

Like noting any mind distraction

A prime moment for their action.

I should not bring myself to hate

The goblins, rather to relate

If I say 'Goblins – Do Not Touch!'

They do not like this very much.

If I remember such to say,

Amazingly, my stuff does stay

Where I placed it so I'm glad.

I suppose they're really not too bad.

But just get lost you goblin horde

'cos I know where my stuff is stored.

Asparagus Tongs

Asparagus tongs, asparagus tongs
The world is full of most terrible wrongs
And yet you just talk of asparagus tongs.

Are they Chinese gangsters with drums and with gongs
Singing incomprehensible songs?
Not those sort of tongs. You're being so silly
Saying just anything, quite willy nilly.

Perhaps I could use them to straighten my hair
Or to put curls in it – make people stare?
I think it's unlikely in this you'd succeed,
In any case, frankly, you haven't the need.

'What are they there for then?' I hear you cry.
'If I don't have them does that mean I'll die?'
All in good time. Death and the rest
But what are they for? I will now do my best

To explain in some detail what they are for
They're to stop the tips falling down onto the floor.
But some people's tips remain tight in their fist
As parting with money they're known to resist.

No, no you duffer. Can't you just see
That which is perfectly obvious to me.
I am talking about the asparagus spear
Which is quite delicious it does appear.

But slippery when with hot butter it's spread.
And if you should drop it you wish you were dead
If you live in the midst of those so special throngs,
Where they actually use asparagus tongs.

Goldfish Perspective

Life in a goldfish bowl is sad.

Restricted space is very bad.

Most times around I merely glide,

But now and then I speed and slide

Bouncing off that concave curve

To see if I still have the nerve.

But I so miss my former friends

As I negotiate the bends.

But being such a fishy fellow

When I try to shout or bellow

What occurs is just absurd.

A stream of bubbles. I'm not heard.

I see the curious look of men's

Faces distorted by the lens

Of my prison's glassy bounds.

Alone with just my watery sounds.

But educated I have been.

Next to my bowl a TV screen

Tells me all I need to know
With the programmes it can show.
I've been to Moscow, Singapore,
Machu Picchu and much more.
Shakespeare, Pinter, all I see
Portrayed by the BBC.
Punchy politics and all
Often hold me in their thrall.
Commentators with their bias,
Politicians – they defy us.
Soccer, Rugger, Cricket too
Exotic creatures from a zoo
Speedy runners in a race.
All that whizzing round in space.
Baking programmes, fancy cakes,
Comedy with umpteen takes.
All this continues day and night
So when it's on it gives delight.

You might be shocked at what I've seen

The other side of the TV screen.

Humans are not sleek like fish

I can imagine that they wish

They didn't have such ugly fins

And unaesthetic outs and ins.

Their behaviour's really odd

Unlike the homely plaice and cod

And when they move it's just so comic.

Whereas I can really frolic

For up and down they need a ladder

Unlike me with my swim bladder

I have to tell you. I can't shirk

But my clear water turns to murk

It's not my choice please rest assured

In such a plight to be immured.

It's rather delicate I know

But in due course it starts to show

And as I slowly dim from sight

My jailers recognise my plight

I have no choice in what I eat

But change for me is no great treat.

They tip me out into a cup

Decant the murk and top me up

With water, fresh from out the tap

They neither think, nor give a rap

That chlorinated water smells.

I can't alert them with my yells

I think they find the bubbles cute.

Sometimes I wish I were a newt

Then I could climb over the rim

But alas, I only swim.

Oh I do miss my dainty meals

Of little fish and tiny eels.

And now I waste away my days,

Exposed in a perpetual glaze.

But it's a two way thing you know.

Some stuff you wouldn't want to show

To others but I have the means

To dish the dirt and spill the beans.

One day I will escape I swear

And down to Fleet Street I will tear.

It may be hard by flip and flop

But mark my words I will not stop

I'll make the effort. Take the trouble

To put my thoughts into a bubble.

If I do that, the battle's won.

I know for sure this can be done

Whether it's by Morse or Braille

I'll take the wind out of their sail.

They're always wanting something new

And I can give a fish-eye view.

Macho Male

Some say that I'm a vicious thug.
This is a horrible sug
Gestion as it's quite untrue.
Friends why should I lie to you?

Though I may lack a daytime job
that doesn't mean that I'm a yob.
But if confronted with a rat
I'll sort him out and that is that.

You bet I can defend my patch
For all aggressors I'm a match.
Yes I have scars upon my face
Though for me that's no disgrace.

I got them in an epic scrap
but you should see the other chap.
I spread joy and I inspire
Often with my own flash choir.

We can't help bursting into song
Sometimes it happens all night long.
When we are out upon the tiles
We just spread happiness and smiles.

It's true I fight and that I'm tough
But some girls like this sort of stuff.
I do my best to treat them right
and keep them happy through the night.

But in the morning I need rousing
after some night-long carousing.
Then I relax under the sun
I've never yet been on the run.

My staff have served me all my life,
An old boy and his lovely wife.
She greets me with her smiling face
and as for him – he knows his place.

I, neither smoke nor drink but I
live on a testosterone high
Conceptualising fatherhood
I've never really understood.

Hygiene matters I am told
On personal grooming I am sold.
My own brand toilet water spray
is very good it lasts all day.

But makes the girls feel rather frisky,
which of course can be quite risky.
So if they really feel the need
Such obligations I must heed.

I have never shirked my duty
I love all forms of feline beauty.
By now you will have worked out that
I am your neighbour's big tom cat.

Customer Service

Important to us is your call

But unfortunately, all

Our operators are at work

But please don't think our job we shirk.

We really do regret delay

You could try later in the day.

A questionnaire we hope you'll fill

So have at hand your current bill

Plus mobile number, date of birth,

Annual salary, what you're worth.

These are simple routine checks

So why those sighs and 'What a neck'?

Remember that you gave assent

That all this data might be sent

To partners whom we carefully choose
In order that you should not lose
The chance to pay into our coffers
For their very special offers.

Passport numbers always help
There really is no need to yelp
Or yell out loud 'This is the bane
Of my life' or cry in pain.

We want to help you so don't fuss.
It's all for you and not for us.
So seriously do we take
Complaints that any clients make.

I churn out platitudes galore,
May I tempt you to some more?

Picture Hanging

It isn't difficult at all

To put a picture on a wall

A fact which cannot be denied

But do you know until you've tried?

Where does it go? Well that depends

On what exactly are your ends.

A watercolour and an oil

Placed adjacent rather spoil

Tranquillity but it could be

That is not the way you see

Things and to you it's right

To put together things that fight.

Plaster ducks upon the wall

Are great for some but not for all

As photographs of tasteful nudes

May not appeal to certain prudes.

It's not that easy. Do you see?

Or am I fussing? Is it me

Who agonises over style

Who checks the inches in each mile?

Alignment works with matching size

Of frames and contents, otherwise

A column based on symmetry

Like a sort of Christmas tree

Is a solution good as most

Though this is hardly worth a boast.

These are just some of the ways

To guide you through this frightful maze.

The question then is of the spacing

That you get with all this placing

Whether 'tis too low or high

Gosh how hard one has to try.

Now I'm afraid I have to speak
About the subject of technique.
A spirit level or just try
To get it right by use of eye?

Do you use cord or binder twine
Or perhaps a bit of fishing line?
Don't be tempted with old string,
Use picture wire. That's the thing.

But now the problems really start
With the attaching of your art
To the wall you had in mind
'cos surfaces can be unkind.

Some sorts of plaster aren't that strong
The art I fear will not last long
Before it crashes to the floor
And you say words like 'What a bore'

Or perhaps it crumbles. Makes a hole
Big enough to take a pole
Perchance the drill just can't get through
This really gets me in a stew.

The fashion's past for picture rails
So I use special mason's nails
Two at a time, side by side
My pictures never slip or slide.

Senior Citizen

If you will kindly turn the page

You'll see that at a certain age

We offer you a hearing aid

They're very good. They're British made.

Or if you wish to take a stick

They're over there. Please take your pick

But when you've finished, put it back

As best you're able, in the rack.

But I will have to take your name

If you require a Zimmer frame.

Should you collapse into a heap

Shall we then cause your heart to leap?

The defib's waiting there to use

We only have to fix the fuse.

Your Doctor's name could be a help

Better now than when you yelp.

I'm sure though that you'll be discreet.
Don't do it here but in the street.
Is this offensive? Dear me, no,
But tell me does it really show?

I thought my bald patch was obscured
But some things just cannot be cured.
The dark sunspecs through which I peep
Are just in case I fall asleep

When I hope they will disguise
The transient closure of my eyes.
The innuendo I've endured
But I'm not blind, please be assured.

I'd flown in on the midnight flight
And partied well into the night.
So to you I might look tired
But sticks are really not required.

And far from me to take the hump
When midway through a free fall jump
I hear 'Are you all right Dad?'
Encouraging to hear, I'm glad,

A cheerful voice of filial care
As we, like birds, fly through the air.
It raises spirits even more
And makes me want to soar and soar.

So should I slip and have a fall
You really won't be blamed at all
Unless I throw a hissy fit –
In which case Sunshine, you're for it!

Bantams

We got some just-hatched bantam chicks. Cute as cute could be
And watched their transformation. What a sight to see.
We wanted hens alone and thought that's what we'd got
Though a cast iron guarantee, sadly there was not.

The prettiest chick among them had made up eyes and all
Chick's legs are not attractive but at least she was quite tall.
Her looks got even better but perhaps a small mistake?
When to our utter horror her voice began to break.

At first 'twas strangulated but it became quite clear
This was no pretty chicken, 'twas a handsome chanticleer.
We shut them up at night and blackouted the boy
Lest his early crowing, our neighbours might annoy.

We thought that all was well until a letter hit the mat
'twas from the Council, threatening action so that I fear was that.
Residential neighbourhoods could not permit loud noise
Except of course from motorbikes and similar boys' toys.

Ignoring this strong letter chanced five thousand pounds of debt.
Reluctant relocation really seemed a better bet.
Arrangements were then made to return him whence he came
Somewhere up in Gloucestershire, I can't recall the name.

His duties were in place there. Nothing left to chance
His future will be rosy. He'll tread a merry dance
There he will be welcome – even if he's loud.
If he can do the business, he'll make his owners proud.

Sunbathing

Digby was a salamander

Sunbathed every day

Something tried to catch him

Digby ran away

But left his tail behind him

What a grisly sight.

A sad and sorry business

But when you're in a plight…

Alphonse was a toad

Who squatted 'neath a fern

Alphonse never sunbathed

But he had an intact stern.

If I had wings

If I had wings and I could fly

I'd flit around up in the sky.

I wouldn't walk or take a stroll,

I'd loop the loop and barrel roll.

And for an extra special stunt

I might even try a bunt.

But to get far above the ground

My muscles I would have to pound.

This unaccustomed exercise

Would certainly increase their size

Until I was obscenely big

Like a sort of flying pig.

Then feathers too I'd have to preen

To keep them functional and clean.

For this I think I'd need a beak

And this could make it hard to speak.

I'm told that feathers make you itch
This doesn't seem much of a pitch
It sounds to me like lots of work
Which truth to tell, I'd rather shirk.

The more about this flying I think
The more towards the ground I sink.
'Tis best by far I'm sure, that I
Should stick to earth and not to sky.

Not Oven Ready

Upon the hottest summer's day I clearly heard a chicken say

'As I swelter in the heat, I look down at my non-webbed feet

Reflecting that I really oughter be afloat upon the water.

I should have been a duck I think, but would I float or would I sink?

The water too, it might be hot, so should I jump or should I not?

Chicken's brains are not equipped for such decisions. We have slipped

Into domestic life, entirely free from stress or strife.

An egg a day is all that's asked and it's with this that we are tasked.

Chicken jalfrezi. That sounds good but I am told it means I'm food.

Oven ready's not for me. I'll join the penguins in the sea.

Deep in the water now unseen, I realise just how daft I've been.

I am drenched right through down to my down

and do believe that I might drown.

I'm just a chick, give me a break. I didn't know what was at stake.

My squawks of protest, cries of need, I greatly fear no one will heed

But to the surface they will float and like an old, abandoned boat

Drift onto some distant shore but by then I'll be no more.'

An Evolutionary Tale

At tadpole stage we swam with ease
And later shone at climbing trees,
But on this evolutionary trail,
At some point we lost our tail.

On meeting friends in park and street
There is a mutual urge to greet,
But now it seems there is a snag,
We lack the wherewithal to wag.
A tricky business, lacking hope
But human beings have to cope.
We learned to talk and write in verse
It may be bad, but could be worse.
Olfactory lamp posts not required
Because we are now satnav wired.
But satnav sometimes gets it wrong,
So we must be alert and strong
In certain countries south of Spain
We could be routed Camel Train.
Next stop day trips to the moon
I do hope this is not too soon.

Jack Spratt

The deposition of human fat was the lifetime study of Dr Spratt.
The appetite, he was to find,
was controlled by more than the human mind.

Jack Spratt could eat no fat, his wife could eat no lean.
They were good for a long-term study,
The best there's ever been.

He grew rather skinny, she inclined to plump.
He disliked hard benches, she had a better rump.

As they became older another difference grew,
He abhorred the cold, but the heat made her go, 'Phew!'
This was rather a tricky one which did produce a frown.
When Jack turned up the heating, she just turned it down.

But in any marriage, there's always give and take,
Really to think otherwise would be a big mistake.

Spring

One vernal Equinoxal morn

I leaped from bed to greet the dawn.

Such unaccustomed exercise

Might well elicit some surprise

An explanation I can bring.

It was of course that wretched spring

It pierced the mattress you know where

I'm much relieved that it stopped there.

Introduction to Mondegreens

Identifying mondegreens is rather like catching exotic butterflies, but they can be preserved in verse rather than being mean with long pins. Just in case you haven't come across them before, I had better explain that a mondegreen is a form of word play involving a misunderstood but still meaningful interpretation of a word or phrase. Its name is derived from a line in the Scottish ballad entitled 'The Bonnie Earl o' Moray'. This commemorates the murder, in 1592, of the Earl of Moray, a contender for the Scottish throne:

'They ha' slain the Earl o' Moray and laid him on the green ...'
Subsequently this was often misinterpreted as 'They ha' slain the Earl o' Moray and Lady Mondegreen.'

I stumbled across mondegreens as a teenager when one of my mother's friends told her she would be unable to come to a meeting planned a week later as the Countess of Ayr was coming to tea. Read on …

The Countess of Ayr

The Countess of Ayr comes to tea

But strictly, between you and me,

There wasn't an Earl and this was no pearl.

The County Surveyor's a 'He'.

Doing Bird

What does 'illegal' mean to you?

If it's 'unlawful'… Nothing new

But perhaps a raptor in a plight

After a rather riotous night?

Canny Scots

Some Highland Scots when in Dunoon

Eat tart and custard with a spoon

But each takes care that nothing's spilt

Down the front of his tartan kilt.

Ecclesiastical Archery

I wonder where that arrow went

I'm sure the wretched thing was bent

Will someone please go to the barrow

And bring to me a Straight and Narrow?

Dressing Down

A wolf in cheap clothing, all tatters and rags

Was down in the gutter looking for fags.

A passing sheep saw him and filled with compassion,

Gave wool from her back, thus starting a fashion.

Devotional

Gladly, the cross-eyed bear

Is in the hymnal I swear

His focus is poor, his balance unsure

His devotion though's beyond compare.

First Aid

I thought the sky looked rather blue

But wasn't quite sure what to do

So I reflected – had a think

I cleared his airway. He turned pink.

Less and Less

I had forgotten I confess

That 'Infra' means not more but less

So In for a Penny, In for a pound

Has a rather fiscal sound.

Best avoided if

Absinthe makes the heart grow fonder

That's enough to make you ponder

But when you know your toes will curl

Will you still give it a whirl?

Snug Solution

A long-felt want's a Winter thing.

It keeps the chill away till Spring

You wrap it round your body twice

And you'll feel warm. That's my advice.

Camping

I rashly promised that I'd glue it

When I got a Round Tuit

'cos feelings get intense in tents

When water leaks through canvas rents.

Ha Ha Grandpa

Your invitation is attached to Grandpa's birthday lunch

It's a landmark birthday so there'll be good food to munch

There's just one stipulation – well, it's really more advice

The old boy says 'No Presents please. Your presence will suffice.'

A Door

I merely asked the French *au pair*

If she would shut the door.

She then became quite amorous

I'm telling you no more.

The Fromes

The Viscountess Frome had booked the best room

For the first week in May

On arrival she found that she had to stand ground

Mike and Tess were expected to stay.

The Allium Clan

Regretfully, each time I try

To cut up onions, I just cry

But portions matter, cold or hot

Take this long thin one – that shallot.

Mondegreen Key

County Surveyor/Countess of Ayr

Illegal/Ill eagle

Tart and/Tartan

Straight and narrow/Straightened arrow

Cheap clothing/Sheep's clothing

Crossed eyed/Cross I'd

The sky/This guy

Infra/In for a

Absinthe/Absence

long felt (emotion)/long felt (material)

A Round Tuit/Around to it

Presence/Presents

Shut the Door/Je t'adore

Viscountess/Mike and Tess

That shallot/That's your lot

And finally…

Taxing

Attacks by tigers are no more

Upon the streets of Singapore

A taxidermist stuffs the pelt

Of polar bears caught in the melt

A tack's a nail that's wide and short

Once used for carpets we were taught

Ataxia affects the nerves

When trying to walk straight, one swerves

A taxi ride is all the rage

For people of a certain age

A tax on sugar we're advised

Will stop us getting oversized.